JAGUAR D-TYPE & XKSS

Andrew Whyte

CONTENTS

Because of the unusual nature of the D-type and XKSS the section headings and content of this book vary from the usual Super Profile format.

Titles in the *Super Profile* series

Austin-Healey 'Frogeye' Sprite (F343)

Ferrari 250GTO (F308)

Ford GT40 (F332)

Jaguar D-Type & XKSS (F371)

Jaguar Mk 2 Saloons (F307)

Lotus Elan (F330)

MGB (F305)

Morris Minor & 1000 (ohv) (F331)

Porsche 911 Carrera (F311)

Further titles in this series will be published at
regular intervals. For information on new titles
please contact your bookseller or write to the
publisher

ISBN 0 85429 371 2

A FOULIS Motoring Book

First published 1983

© **Haynes Publishing Group**

Published by:
Haynes Publishing Group
Sparkford, Yeovil,
Somerset BA22 7JJ

Distributed in USA by:
Haynes Publications Inc.
861 Lawrence Drive, Newbury
Park, California 91320, USA

Editor: Rod Grainger
Dust jacket design: Rowland Smith
Page Layout: Graham Thompson
Dust jacket colour picture: Pit scene
from the Le Mans 50th anniversary
historic car race – won by Anthony
Bamford's ex *Ecurie Ecosse* long-nose
D-Type. Martin Morris's D-Type
(pictured) came third. Photograph
courtesy of Paul Skilleter.
Colour photographs: Paul Skilleter
Road tests: Courtesy of *Motor,
Autosport, Autocar* and *Punch*
Printed in England by: J.H.Haynes &
Co. Ltd

FOREWORD

The D-type Jaguar has a very special place in history.

Firstly it was built for a specific purpose, and its achievement of the objective was quite outstanding. It was designed to carry on where the C-type left off – as a Le Mans winner *par excellence.* Le Mans is the most famous race in the world, and to succeed at Le Mans was to succeed in world markets. The D-type won three times in a row, and became an instant "classic". Its comparative lack of success elsewhere serves to emphasise Jaguar's singleness of purpose when creating it.

Secondly the D-type showed that, in the 1950s, the development of automobile engineering was still at a stage where the competition car of the day led logically to the road car of the morrow. The subsequent E-type Jaguar (subject of a separate *Super Profile*) illustrates the point perfectly.

Thirdly, it is generally agreed that its exquisite lines make the D-type a contender for the "most beautiful car" stakes. This has led not only to high prices and superb standards of restoration, but also to the manufacture of two series of modern cars looking so similar to the original that they can be mistaken for it at first glance. It has even led to the construction of complete cars very nearly to original specification.

One of the chief tasks of this book is to help clarify the various versions of the D-type and its more modern "lookalike" equivalents. In a sense, the D-type is an easier car than some to deal with, because the origin of each car is known. Recent history can be another matter, and the only general advice for the researcher is to establish fact as far as possible, before declaring it as such. Even the interchange of parts between works cars, all those years ago, has led to doubts over identity today. Another important point to remember is the ease with which myths may be perpetuated. No book can be used as a complete guide for D-type buyer, but it is hoped that this one will provide some useful points of reference.

I am very grateful to Jaguar Cars Limited for the use of pictures and research material, and to the Jaguar Specialists' Association – in particular Guy Black and Bryan Wingfield whose combination of engineering skill and enthusiasm has given them exceptional experience in the re-creation and renovation of the "D". Thanks are due to Martin Morris, so often the only D-type campaigner in historic car racing in the 1970s, and to Len Pritchard of Williams and Pritchard – probably the first firm in the field of D-type rebuilds – for discussing the subject at length.

Michael Barker of the Midland Motor Museum, Roger Clinkscales, Alan Hodge and their colleagues at Jaguar, Bob Smith of RS Panels, and Michael Ware of the National Motor Museum were most co-operative as regards photography. Here I should like to say how much I appreciate the photographic help I had from Paul Skilleter. Many Jaguar people have lent their experience willingly and engine specialists Ron Beaty and George Hodge were particularly helpful.

Many other people have added to my own Jaguar experience during the long years of research which led to my two large-scale Haynes books on Jaguar's complete competition history. The first of these was published in 1982, and covers the period up to and including 1953. The second volume brings the story up to date. A feature of the double volume is a comprehensive, illustrated, section on each individual C-type and D-type, by chassis number, with early competition history listed for each, where verified.

In this *Super Profile*, too, will be found a list of every D-type together with the comments of the most active restorer, Guy Black, and myself. If any readers would like to contribute or obtain further information on D-type history, I shall be pleased to hear from them; they might be *just* in time to add something to the second of the major works now in preparation and scheduled to be published in 1984.

Meantime, let me introduce the wonderful D-type Jaguar – one of the proudest, most exciting, and best engineered competition cars ever seen.

Andrew Whyte

HISTORY & EVOLUTION

Family Tree

There is a strong argument for the idea that the D-type is the epitome of "Jaguar" past, present and – who knows? – future.

William Lyons never planned for his company to take part in motor-racing. He had embarked on business life in 1922 with his partner William Walmsley making "Swallow" sidecars, and soon got to know the seamier side of motor sport when he found a rival trying to monopolise the Isle of Man races by persuading "Swallow" runners to change sidecars for another make. (Lyons caught-on quickly, and put a stop to that).

Later, Swallow made special bodies for everyday makes of car; but only one, the Wolseley Hornet Special, could be called a "sports" car. The same applied to the first "SS" cars, announced in 1931.

It was not until Spring 1935 that Lyons produced his first true sports car – an attractive short-wheelbase two-seater, the SS 90. Almost simultaneously, he created an engineering department of his own by "head-hunting" William Heynes whose work at Humber was much admired.

Up to this time the SS company had been in the coachbuilding trade, putting up with whatever mechanical components were readily available.

It is true that Standard had agreed to supply a special underslung version of their six-cylinder chassis to SS, and that Harry Weslake was already well on the way to converting the Standard engine from SV to OHV, exclusively for Lyons. Nevertheless, the work done by Heynes in the summer of 1935 was prodigious and, that Autumn, the first SS "Jaguar" range was announced. The range included the "100" 2-seater, using the "90" body, the ohv engine, and many chassis improvements.

The "100" became a competitive rally car, due to its excellent straight-line performance, its manoeuvrability, and its basic reliability which enabled it to make best performance in two Alpine Trials and in two RAC Rallies.

Despite its superb looks, the "100" was not in the least aerodynamic, so its acceleration fell away badly at higher speeds. Moreover, its handling at racing speeds was not as nimble as that of the BMW 328 – Europe's other great bargain sports car of the new 100mph class. Sir William Lyons has made no secret of the fact that he paid an entrant to withdraw from the 1938 RAC TT – Britain's major production-car race – rather than risk showing the new Jaguar marque in a poor light. (In 1939 the problem did not arise, because of the outbreak of war).

"SS" became "Jaguar" in 1945, and three years later hit the headlines at London's first postwar motor show with the sleek "XK" sports car; but it was essentially a sports car *for the road* – more specifically still, for the boulevards of California where comfort and soft-springing were the norm, and where Lyons correctly foresaw a great potential market for Jaguar.

Then, at Silverstone in August 1949, the *Daily Express* sponsored a one-hour production-car race at the BRDC's International Trophy meeting. It would have been difficult to find an excuse to avoid taking part and, shortly beforehand, Bill Heynes' chief development engineer, Walter Hassan, ran a day's testing at the Silverstone circuit. Despite Hassan's reports of cracked brake drums due to expansion, of excessive brake lining wear and roughness, and of other items calling for further major development, Lyons decided to accede to the *Express's* pressure and entered three of the new XK 120s.

Had one of them not spun out of the lead with a puncture (due, it was thought, to the body fouling a rear tyre) the Jaguars would have finished 1,2, and 3. As it was, they came first and second. From then on, there was little that could stem the tide, and few people analysed the Silverstone result, which had not in fact been *such* a walkover; a Frazer Nash (designed largely on BMW lines) had finished well within sight of the Jaguars.

About to leave Jaguar to join Coventry Climax, Hassan could afford some bluntness in a memorandum of response to a Lyons enquiry. The planned TT race revival had been put off for a year; Lyons wanted to win it, now that postwar production of Jaguars was rising rapidly. "Our sales are certain, from price and performance only", wrote the former Bentley boy. "I should have thought that the firm could well leave competition alone this year, develop a competition model that would sell at some increased price, then have a go the following year if it is considered desirable."

Intentionally or otherwise, William Lyons heeded Walter Hassan's words of wisdom, delivered at the end of 1949. The XK120C or C-type Jaguar was created in the latter part of 1950 and testing began early in 1951. In June that year it appeared in public for the first time at Le Mans for the World's most famous race, the 24-hour *Grand Prix d'Endurance.* It won!

From tentative beginnings

Jaguar were, suddenly, Britain's big international sports-car race winners — the first on this scale since the Bentley days.

Le Mans was now *the* objective, but Jaguar made the classic mistake of incorporating untried "improvements" to the C-type, which meant failure of the whole team in 1952.

1953 brought real planning to the Jaguar competition programme, however. There were two lines of attack. One was via the C-type, improving its performance (through more power and less weight) and its braking (by the pioneering use of Dunlop's aircraft-type discs fitted to all four roadwheels). The other route was a more steamlined, more compact, car with hints of Alfa Romeo's *disco volante* in its shape. Pictures of this experimental Jaguar were issued to the press in early June to permit conjecture for the future, but it was the familiar C-type in its revised form which annihilated the very strong 1953 Le Mans opposition.

The un-named Jaguar re-appeared three times. In October 1953 it was taken to the Ostende-Bruxelles motorway, where Jaguar test engineer Norman Dewis crouched under a Slingsby glider bubble and, despite a slight misfire, averaged 178.383mph for a mean mile. The best run was a "flying" kilometre at 179.817mph.

Body design expert Malcolm Sayer, formerly of Bristol aircraft, referred to this machine as the "XK120C Mk II" when reporting on it as being obviously sufficiently stable for higher speeds than those obtained.

This "Mk II" C-type appeared again in the following spring for wheel and tyre tests at Reims (together with a more conventional C-type); and finally for a private Le Mans test session, which also marked the first public appearance of the D-type.

It wasn't called "D" to start with. The name just happened. From the heavy "boulevard"

sports-car — the XK120, which Hassan had warned would not make a "racer" — had come the "C". (The letter had stood for "Competition"). It had used many XK120 parts, but its all-tube spaceframe and its aerodynamic body — which bore *some* small resemblance to the production version — had set it apart, and made it a Le Mans winner.

Now the opposition was hotting up, and the C-type had reached its peak of development. It seemed natural enough, in the experimental and competition departments, to refer to the hush-hush new car as the "D-type" in that spring of 1954.

Concept

"With a little less adherence to production components and a little less emphasis on the considerations of Le Mans, the D-type could have been a world-beater on any circuit". That is the view of John Wyer who ran the Aston Martin team in its heyday, and was later to be of such assistance with the Ford racing effort.

The speed and reliability needed to win Le Mans, plus the comfort and safety of the drivers — these were the main considerations of Jaguar who were racing to promote world sales that were moving quickly towards the 20,000 a year mark, whereas Wyer's company was still a plaything of its saviour David Brown. Of course Aston Martin made fine cars, but in relatively small quantities.

The first "adherence to production" was in the engine. The XK engine had, in fact, been in production for five years when the D-type appeared. It had been announced for the launch of the XK120 sports car, and had powered the Mark Seven — Jaguar's first 100mph saloon — since its debut late in 1950.

The XK engine (still very

much in production 35 years after it first appeared!) was a splendid team effort. William Lyons established the principle of a powerful, efficient engine that also looked good when you opened the bonnet. Bill Heynes and his top engineers — Walter Hassan (development) and Claude Baily (design) — put the idea into practice, with the help of the independent consultant gas flow expert, Harry Weslake.

For the D-type, there were some important changes to the twin overhead camshaft, seven-bearing, steel-block, alloy-head, 3441cc six-cylinder engine. The biggest difference enabled the car's frontal area to be reduced from the C-type's 13.8 square feet down to 12.5 for the new car. That alteration was from wet to dry sump lubrication. Sump depth was halved and, with the engine mounted at eight degrees from the vertical, the bonnet line with its offset hump was exceptionally low.

An oil-cooler was fitted and the oil tank was mounted on the left of the car, ahead of the bulkhead. The pressure pump was to the right of the engine block; the scavenge pump to the left.

Another factor in height reduction was the separation of header tank from radiator; both were made of aluminium.

The engine was fitted with triple horizontal-barrel Weber carburetters, a set-up which had proved most successful on the works C-types at Le Mans in 1953. Gross power output was about 245bhp at 5750rpm.

Another feature which had been tried on the last of the C-types was the triple-plate clutch. There wasn't a flywheel, so the outer rim of the clutch casing served as the starter ring. The gearbox was virtually all new, all-Jaguar, and all-synchromesh.

Newest of all was the design of the D-type's structure — Jaguar's first true *monocoque*. While the C-type had been born in the era of the "riding mechanic" and had been raced in this form, the "passenger" was considered superfluous to the design of the D-type – but of course regulations insisted upon a second seat. So it was that the 18-gauge elliptical body was devised. Like a piece of tube lying on its side, this magnesium alloy centre section was given two apertures – one on the right for the driver and the other, much smaller, for the mythical passenger. The ends of the cockpit were given effective lids, or bulkheads. Welded to this structure was a tubular front subframe designed to carry the engine and the double-wishbone independent front suspension, featuring longitudinal torsion bars with a scale for instant ride-height adjustment. The rear torsion bar was transverse and there were four sturdy trailing links from the back of the cockpit to locate the regular, live, Salisbury axle, lateral movement of which was controlled by a central A-bracket.

While the rear end was very much a "trailing" member, the front subframe and the monocoque centre-section were as one. Indeed on early models the engine subframe was welded to the centre section. On production and later works cars it was bolted for easy detachment. Steering was rack-and-pinion.

Thanks to Dunlop's Joe Wright, Jaguar were well ahead on disc brake development, having first raced with this aero-industry system as early as Easter 1952. Not every driver took gladly to the effect on the foot-pedal of the transmission-driven Plessey brake servo, but few disputed the efficiency of the discs. On the simple principle of 60/40 front to rear distribution, the early D-types still had three pairs of pads at the front and two at the rear. Dunlop also provided the alloy centre-lock wheels, which had been tested at Reims and selected following the break-up of spokes on the wire-wheeled 1953 C-types.

The D-type shape was a beautiful flowing of curves. Under

the rear were housed a spare wheel tray and two flexible fuel tanks, which had been a feature of the last (1953) works C-types.

Whereas the C-type's dry weight had been about 18¾cwt (reduced to 18cwt in the three 1953 works team "lightweight" cars), the new D-type was down to a respectable 17¼cwt.

The "private" test session at Le Mans in May 1954 was not really very private. Use of the circuit had been obtained only by virtue of its closure to traffic for a speed test forming part of a rally, so it was a group of French enthusiasts who first saw the D-type in action, whereas Britishers at the Silverstone international meeting a few days later had to make do with seeing last year's C-type coming 3rd and 4th in miserable conditions.

Le Mans testing was brief, but the few laps covered showed that the D-type was competitive with the known opposition. Incidentally, the "C-type MK II" (which had SU fuel-injection fitted for the occasion) never appeared in public again, and vanished without escaping from Coventry.

A batch of six D-types was built in 1954 – four of them, the prototype (now housed at the National Motor Museum, Beaulieu) and three team cars being completed in time for the 24-hour race in June.

For 1955, the D-type remained essentially unchanged, the new Le Mans cars being based on the production version for which a small assembly line was set up that Summer. The biggest difference was in a simplification of the front subframe to cockpit relationship. The 1955 subframe was made of steel and, where it extended into the cockpit area, the two upper members were cut short and new tubes angled downwards to meet the lower members near where they terminated against the rear bulkhead. Several fairly minor bumps at Le Mans (and on the road subsequently) had shown how

difficult it was to work on the 1954 D-type, because the frame and the cockpit were welded together. On all but the original six cars, therefore, these two main structural items were bolted together. There were six bolts through each frame outrigger (thus totalling twelve through the front bulkhead) and four bolts through the rear bulkhead and the back of the frame, plus a whole series along the floor. The outcome was better serviceability, and more space inside.

A further detail improvement was the mounting of the water radiator and adjacent oil cooler on a replaceable, quick-change, frame extension, with a view to aiding "on the spot" repair work in the event of slight front end damage of the type often experienced in racing.

Production cars kept the 1954 "works" engine, which produced about 245bhp. The 1955 works cars were given larger valves and, after the expert fettling talents of Weslake in Rye, Sussex, (still consultants to Jaguar) and Jack Emerson at the works, these engines delivered a gross output of 270bhp. The increased valve sizes did, however, mean some redesigning of the cylinder head. The included angle between valve stems was normally 70 degrees; the 1955 works D-types were the first Jaguars to have what became known as the "35/40 head", a term illustrating the addition of five degrees to the exhaust valve angle (from the engine vertical) to give the necessary clearances.

An optional extra on production D-types was the fin which had been fitted to the headrests of the 1954 team cars. Five new works cars for 1955, however, were given extra-long nosepieces incorporating brake-cooling ducts each side; they also had wrap-round windscreens terminating at the headrest. The fins of these cars were more permanent and extended to the extreme rear. Further smoothness of line was added by bringing the exhaust pipes out at the rear, instead of the nearside.

1956 Le Mans regulations required manufacturers of over-2.5-litre cars, to declare their intention to manufacture 100 similar vehicles. There were also new Le Mans rules which made it necessary to fit a full-width windscreen and a door on the nearside, but only a few of the production cars were so modified, after sale. The fuel-injection and other permitted experimental works fitments were not offered to private owners. Alfred Momo, who prepared the American team cars (a Briggs Cunningham project) introduced the "3.8" idea, and Jaguar adopted it; but that was *after* all D-types – works and otherwise – had been built. It was, however, a works 3.8-litre fuel-injected engine, developing nearly 300bhp, which the private *Ecurie Ecosse* team used in an ex-factory 1956 car to win at Le Mans in 1957 – the marque's fifth and final victory in the 24-hour marathon for which the D-type had been designed. Some privately owned cars acquired 3.8-litre engines, though not always authentic "D" conversions. The only engine size for any D-type *to original specification* is the regular XK figure of 3441 to 3442cc.

The XKSS

During 1955 and 1956, Jaguar continued to build D-types, listing them at £3,878 in the UK, though most were exported. By the Winter of 1956/57 production was in sight of the promised hundred when it was decided to convert the unsold ones into a new model – the Jaguar "XKSS". The Sports Car Club of America listed it initially as a production car, as accepted for racing, but quickly deleted it again – rightly putting it with the D-type in the "modified" category.

The XKSS was announced in January 1957. It consisted of a D-type with specially-made windscreen, a folding soft-top, a nearside door, side curtains, a luggage grid on the tail, and some extra trim inside. Gone were the headrest and the stressed alloy sheeting which had formed the deck between the seats of the original. It was a thoroughly professional conversion; nonetheless it did *look* like a conversion.

In February 1957, several cars in the course of transformation from D to XKSS were lost in a fire which swept through a third of the main Browns Lane, Coventry, assembly plant. In the end, only 16 XKSSs were built as new cars. Most went to the USA, where the list price was 6900 dollars. There have been several subsequent conversions to (and from) XKSS.

In the end, 87 D-types (*including* the 16 XKSSs) were completed by Jaguar – not very far short of that goal of a hundred. (Thanks to today's "reproduction trade", it is probable that the "century" has now been reached!)

Even before the fire, Jaguar had announced its intention to withdraw from sports-car racing as a works team. 1957 was, however, the year in which the Lister-Jaguar leapt to prominence. With the success of Lister Engineering of Cambridge, and the running of D-types (to be succeeded by Lister-Jaguars) by Cunningham in America and *Ecurie Ecosse* for Britain, Jaguar continued to develop the XK engine as a competition unit for some time after its own withdrawal from racing.

Competition

Being designed, like the C-type, as a car for Le Mans naturally the D-type made its debut there. This was the regular pattern, no matter how hard the British Racing Drivers' Club and the *Daily Express* tried to persuade Jaguar to bring this latest model to Silverstone in May 1954.

The main opposition came from Ferrari, whose 4.9-litre monster wielded by the brave Froilan Gonzalez gave notice of its intentions by winning the Silverstone sports-car race quite easily despite atrocious conditions.

In June, the weather at Le Mans was just as bad. The Jaguar team lost time due to misfiring, caused by fuel filters that were proving too small; the filters were discarded and the problem solved. Two of the cars later retired – one with loss of brakes, the other with loss of gears (leading to engine trouble) but the other one boomed its way right through the 24 hours. The drivers were Duncan Hamilton and Tony Rolt, seasoned campaigners and victors in the lightweight C-type the year before, and they proved a brilliant pair once again. Even more brilliant, however, was Froilan Gonzalez – co-driver with Maurice Trintignant in the only surviving 4.9 Ferrari – who maintained sufficient control of the race to survive a frighteningly long pit stop and still win; but the new D-type Jaguar was not disgraced on its debut, less than two minutes behind the Ferrari in one of the closest finishes Le Mans has ever seen.

The D-type's second race appearance was at Reims, for the 12-hour race in July. This time there was no doubt about the winners. Team leaders Stirling Moss and Peter Walker led this race (as they had done before retiring at Le Mans) only to be forced out with propshaft failure. Rolt and Hamilton lost time in the pits after being rammed from behind – a disadvantage of discs? – but recovered to come second behind Peter Whitehead and Ken Wharton whose victory was a convincing one. It should be added, though, that the opposition at Reims was never as strong as it was at Le Mans.

Two D-types were converted to 2½-litres for the Tourist Trophy race at Dundrod in September, and one of them came fifth despite an unscheduled tyre change. The other broke (though it was coaxed across the finishing line), and the only 3½ had mechanical trouble too.

Stirling Moss was soon lost to Mercedes-Benz; but 1955 began well nevertheless. A lone 1954 D-type was sent to Sebring, Florida, for the 12-hour race. Overseen by Briggs Cunningham – who would soon give up making his own cars and run a D-type team instead – the Jaguar came in first, driven by Mike Hawthorn and the American Phil Walters.

As the 1954 cars began winning in private hands, Jaguar returned to Le Mans for the 1955 race with the even-more-purposeful-looking "long-nose" car. It had all the makings of a great race between Jaguar, Ferrari, and Mercedes. Then one of the German cars crashed heavily, killing many spectators in racing's worst-ever catastrophe; that was in the third hour of the race, well before dusk. Early next morning the Mercedes-Benz team withdrew and returned to Germany. With the Ferraris in trouble, it was a hollow victory for Mike Hawthorn, Ivor Bueb, and Jaguar.

Le Mans was held at a later date in 1956, to allow for improvements to the circuit. Even with the extra frontal area caused by the new wide screen, *and* an effective fuel consumption limit, the works D-types looked set for a disciplined drive to the chequered flag. Two cars crashed in drizzle five minutes after the start, and the third lost many laps before a cracked pipe in the new fuel-injection system was located. It caught up to 6th.

Privately-entered D-types rose to the occasion, however, and took 1st and 4th places. The winning car was driven for David Murray's well-managed *Ecurie Ecosse* team by Ron Flockhart and Ninian Sanderson. (The last victory for the works team was in the 1956 Reims 12-hour race).

At the end of the season, the Scottish team acquired three "long-nose" works cars and in 1957 came 1st *and 2nd* at Le Mans to make it a hat-trick for the D-type, and five Jaguar wins there altogether! Flockhart and Bueb drove the winning car which had a works 300bhp fuel-injection 3.8 engine; Lawrence and Sanderson came 2nd on 3.4-litres and triple Weber carburetters. Works-prepared French and Belgian entered production D-types came 3rd and 4th in this fine, but final, demonstration of D-type dominance on the circuit for which it was designed.

For several years from 1958, the regulations demanded a top limit of 3-litres on Le Mans entries. XK engines were adapted by the works and by *Ecurie Ecosse* but neither version was successful. The D had had its day ...

Even if it was not at its best on uneven or twisting courses, the D-type did have many moments of glory, and car-by-car details of its achievements worldwide – works, "assisted", and private – will be found in my book *Jaguar Sports Racing and Works Competition Cars from 1954* which will be published by Haynes in 1984.

COPY CARS & RE-CREATIONS

If this book is to provide information not only for the enthusiast but for the prospective purchaser, then "copy cars" must be included too.

Like most great competition machines of its era, the D-type Jaguar went through a lengthy period – probably a decade or so – in which it was just another obsolete car wanted by only a few collectors.

The few Americans still racing the D-type in the 1960s tended to fit one of their indigenous V8 engines to try and stay competitive. This idea was bad at the time—as it is in retrospect—because it meant cutting into the front subframe. Therefore the manner of rebuild or renewal of this key item for restoration purposes is important from two points of view – safety and authenticity. The stamping of the chassis number on top of the front shock-absorber mounts is a guide to, but not always proof of, originality now that historic car prices have rocketed.

The central monocoque is the other important base upon which the D-type is built.

The owner of a subframe and a monocoque, known to have left the Jaguar factory attached to one another, is well on the way to being the owner of a genuine D-type – by today's standards.

It should be stated here that the world of the "classic" car is a free world, whose inhabitants must feel free to do exactly as they please. This is as life *should* be; but the D-type is also a classic illustration of the need for any purchaser to have an enquiring mind as well as a large wallet.

There are few enough D-types, so the serious potential owner is likely to know what to ask and how to find the answer. The person looking for a genuine original can usually identify it, warts and all—for it is certain it will not be perfect by any means. He should also find a *true* replica acceptable. A replica, according to the excellent *Chambers Twentieth Century Dictionary,* is "a duplicate, properly one by the original artist: a facsimile: a repeat." Few D-types will be found to have all original components. To make new ones to the manufacturer's standard is an accepted fact of the historic car business. How else could there be so many fine veteran and vintage cars in running order today?

The problem of identity can still remain, when it comes to numbering. In the case of a competition car, identification numbers are important if the racing history is considered as part of the vehicle's intrinsic value; yet even the works, let alone private owners, frequently changed components during a racing season or prior to sale. Famous registration numbers, again, are only a guide in some circumstances.

Perhaps the biggest quandary would be the hypothetical case of two or more cars sharing claim to a single identity. When and if that happens, the seeker must do his or her own deep research and judge accordingly. Fortunately, the specialised nature of the work has now limited the true expertise to a few well-known and reputable concerns. (Here it should be added that much of this expertise also covers the field of the C-type Jaguar).

Having mentioned the word "replica" in its (hopefully) correct context, it is essential to pay tribute to the cars which *look* like D-types, but do not pretend to be D-types, except in general appearance. There have been several false starts and "one-offs", but two successful companies have emerged in this field. It is not the intention of either firm to misuse the term "replica". It is, simply, impossible to describe in one word a car built to look like another—and to the same high engineering standards—yet at the same time give it a distinctly different beneath-the-surface specification. It is not reasonable to say that these fine cars called the "Lynx" and the "Deetype" are merely in the spirit of the D-type; thus they are often *described* as "replicas", and understanding of this usage has become universal. Only we nitpicking authors seem to have occasional trouble on such trifling matters as semantics.

The restoration of D-types has of course been a continuous process ever since they went out of production. In the early days, the factory service department undertook such work. Even today, some of the racing team staff of the 1950s work for Jaguar; several of those who have retired are still delighted to share their knowledge, though this is naturally a matter of establishing personal contact.

Naturally too, in these changed times, there are more appropriate places to go for specialised restorative work. The original D-type bodies were made by Abbey Panels of Coventry (later to make the major panels for the E-type), but the first company to be given a whole series of D-type replacement orders was the North London firm of Williams and Pritchard, whose experience in the field of racing body production and reproduction has earned them a worldwide reputation for accurate work. When the late Nigel Moores (who entered races as "Willie Eckerslyke") made the collecting of D-type Jaguars a serious hobby, it was Williams and Pritchard who re-created those endlessly curving shapes for him.

Although they would soon pull out of any direct involvement, Charles Williams and Len Pritchard – by their existing work – did create the idea of the Deetype, and they supplied Lynx of East Sussex with *their* first complete copy of the nose, centre section and tail of the beautiful D-type Jaguar, too. Approaches to the firm from Deetype and Lynx were coincidental, and virtually simultaneous.

The press preview for London's 1975 Speedshow (formerly The Racing Car Show) at Olympia took place on 31st December, 1974, and the first news story of the copy-cars was of their confrontation – for both of them appeared in the exhibition hall. The Deetype, was to have been marketed by the first customers, Robert Lamplough and his brother-in-law Alastair Walker of Sidney Marcus Ltd., though its concept was the work of Bryan Wingfield – trained at Glasgow University and Albion Motors, later with Ford – who holds the company name "Deetype Replicas". That first car had a long-nose body based upon the 1955 works Le Mans shape, complete with wrap-round windscreen. It used modern mechanical components, but the flavour of the original Jaguar lived on in the use of a complete Salisbury 4HA rear axle unit, and a subframe which passed through to the rear of the monocoque.

SPECIFICATION

Jaguar D-type and XKSS

Type designation	As above
Built	At Jaguar Cars Ltd., Browns Lane, Allesley, Coventry

Numbers made (all RHD)

1954 works cars:	6	(Chassis XKD 401 to 406)
1955 long-nose cars:	5	(Chassis XKD 504 to 508)
1955/6 production cars:	54	(Chassis Series '500')*
1956 long-nose cars:	6	(Chassis XKD 601 to 606)
1957 XKSS models:	16	(Chassis Series '700')*
Total:	87	

*See chassis list for details of '500' and '700' series. (It should be recorded that the first six cars were originally prefixed 'XKC', before the D-type name was coined.)

Drive configuration	Front engine; rear wheel drive.
Engine	Jaguar XK, 6-cylinder, 2 ohc; alloy head with hemispherical combustion chambers; cast iron cylinder block; 3442cc; 83mm bore and 106mm stroke standard, except for 1954 TT (two cars of 2482cc, 83x76.5mm, for handicap reasons). 3.8-litre and 3.0-litre engines used only after works withdrawal from racing.
Engine power (gross)	245 to 250bhp between 5750 & 6000rpm on 1954 and prod. cars. 265 to 270bhp between 5750 & 6000rpm on 1955 works cars. 272 to 277bhp between 5750 & 6000rpm on 1956 works cars (300+ bhp from works-prepared 3781cc engines in 1957 season.)
Fuel supply	Twin SU pumps from flexible tanks in tail; total capacity 37 gals std.; carburation through three twin-choke DC03 Weber carburetters. (Fuel injection on some late works cars was Lucas mechanical, apart from one car fitted with an SU fuel-injection system.)
Transmission	Four-speed all-synchromesh gearbox and triple-plate Borg & Beck clutch to hypoid bevel final drive with 3.54 to 1 or alternative ratio. The highest regular works Le Mans ratio was 2.69 to 1 (ZF diff.) Typical

ratios as follows:
2.93 to 1 giving 3450rpm in top gear at 100mph.
3.31 to 1 giving 3900rpm in top gear at 100mph.
3.54 to 1 giving 4170rpm in top gear at 100mph.
3.92 to 1 giving 4630rpm in top gear at 100mph.
(4.09 to 1, 4.27 to 1, and 4.55 to 1 also offered).

Braking/Steering	Dunlop disc brakes all round; rack and pinion steering.
Electrics/Instruments	12 volt system, 38 amp/hour at 10 hour rate or 43 amp hour at 20 hour rate. Tachometer oil pressure, and water temperature gauges.
Wheels/Tyres	Dunlop — 16x5$\frac{1}{2}$K light alloy wheels, 6.50 — 16 racing tyres.
Suspension	IFS by wishbones & torsion bars; live rear axle with trailing links and transverse torsion bar.
Main dimensions	Standard length (1954 and prod.): 12ft.10in. Estimated length (XKSS, inc. bumpers): 13ft.1in. Length 1955/56 works cars (long nose): 13ft.5$\frac{1}{2}$in. Height over fin (prod. optional): 3ft.8in. Height over fin (1955/56 works): 3ft.9in. Wheelbase: 7ft.6$\frac{1}{2}$in. Width: 5ft.5$\frac{1}{2}$in. Front track: 4ft.2in. Rear track: 4ft.0in. Scuttle height: 2ft.7$\frac{1}{2}$in.

Deetype and Lynx models

Type Designation	**Deetype**	**Lynx**
Built	Deetype Replicas Ltd., South Gibcracks Farm, Bicknacre Road, East Hanningfield, Chelmsford, Essex, England.	Lynx Motor Co. Ltd., Unit 8, Castleham Road, Castleham Industrial Estate, St. Leonards-on-Sea, East Sussex, England.
Numbers made (all RHD)	13 between 1974 and 1983.	22 between 1974 and 1983.
Drive configuration	Front engine; rear wheel drive.	Front engine; rear wheel drive.
Engine	Jaguar XK, modified to customer's specification, from 3.4 to 4.5-litres, the latter being a Forward Engineering unit giving some 340bhp.	Jaguar XK, modified to customer's specification, usually 3.8 or 4.2 E-type, fitted with Weber carburetters; dry sump conversion optional.
Transmission	Jaguar production-type four-speed all-synchro.	Jaguar production-type four-speed all-synchro.
Braking	Modern disc braking all round; outboard rear.	Modern disc braking all round; inboard rear.

Wheels/tyres	15-inch dia. composite alloy/steel-rimmed, with modern road or race tyres.	15-inch dia. composite alloy/steel-rimmed, with modern road or race tyres.
Suspension	Basically E-type at the front; live rear axle held by four radius arms as D-type, but sprung by coil/damper units (no transverse torsion bar).	Virtually standard E-type front and rear, being independent all-round, with the rear discs mounted inboard.
Structure	E-type front subframe extended by inclusion of fabricated pyramid, passing through cockpit area, adds D-type authenticity. Choice of specification includes short or long nose.	E-type front subframe mounted (like the E-type) to the bulkhead; E-type rear subframe too. Like the Deetype, the Lynx follows D-type shape closely, long and short nose versions and XKSS style being offered.

INDIVIDUAL CARS BY CHASSIS NUMBER

Individual Cars by Chassis Number

Chassis (XKD)	Brief details of first destination	Lynx involvement and 1982 location (in italics). Author's comments (in normal type)
401	Works prototype.	Still Jaguar-owned, based at National Motor Museum, Beaulieu.
402	1954 works Le Mans team car.	*Spares, Australia.* Owner, John Goddard.
403	1954 works Le Mans team car.	*Purchased by Lynx and rebuilt; UK sale.*
404	1954 works Le Mans team car.	*Spares, UK.* Owner, Martin Morris.
405	1954 works car (never sold).	More information sought by author.
406	1954 works car ('55 Sebring).	*Spares, UK.*
501	Ecurie Ecosse, May '55.	*Spares, UK.* '56 Le Mans winner.
502	Ecurie Ecosse, May '55.	*Total Rebuild, UK.* Much modified in interim.
503	Belgian team, works prep.	3rd at Le Mans '55, later to USA
504*	1955 works Le Mans team car.	*Total rebuild, UK.* See footnote.
505*	1955 works Le Mans team car.	*New car built around frame.* See XKD 601 and footnote.
506*	1955 works Le Mans team car.	*Major rebuild work, France.* Works to Cunningham, USA '56.
507*	1955 works Le Mans team car.	Raced Le Mans '55 as Cunningham car, then to USA.
508*	1955 works Le Mans spare car.	Works to Cunningham, USA '56.
509	First true production car.	Exported new to California.
510	Richard Wilkins, UK.	*Spares, Australia.* Twice wrecked; sold '82; see text.
511	Capt. Ian Baillie, UK.	On show in excellent Chipping Campden collection.
512	Lord Louth, UK to Africa.	Collection of the late Nigel Moores.
513	French team, works prep.	*Ex-Michelotti, total reconstruction, USA.* '63 Geneva car.
514	Sir Robert Ropner, UK.	*Spares, Denmark.* Sommer collection, near Copenhagen.
515	Col. Ronald Hoare, UK.	Collection of the late Nigel Moores.
516	Cdr. Jack Rutherford, USA.	*Major servicing and spares, UK.*

517	Alex McMillan, UK.	Raced '58 by Jim Clark; later B.Corser & W.Tuckett.
518	Peter Blond, UK.	Later Clive Lacey.
519	Bill Krause, USA.	One of the first to have a V8 fitted to stay competitive.
520	Bib Stillwell, Australia.	*Major overhaul, sold by Lynx to Jersey customer.*
521	Alfonso Gomez Mena, Cuba.	Appeared at Sebring, '56.
522	1955 Los Angeles show car.	Owned in recent years by Tom Groskritz, USA.
523	To USA	*Spares, USA.*
524	To USA	Recent info sought.
525	Briggs Cunningham, USA.	Cunningham's ''personal''—as opposed to ''team''—car.
526	Cyril Anderson, Australia.	*Spares, USA.* Raced by Bill Pitt in Australia.
527	Jerry Austin, USA.	Back in UK, early '70s.
528	Pearce Woods, USA.	*Spares and repairs, USA.*
529	Tage Hansen, USA.	*Spares and repairs, USA.* Raced by Walt Hansgen, '56.
530	Curt Lincoln, Finland.	Collection of the late Nigel Moores.
531	Jack Douglas, USA.	*Spares and repairs, USA.* With Tom Groskritz many years.
532	Jack Parker, Australia.	Many years in Bob Jane's collection.
533	M. Monnoyeur, France.	Converted to XKSS at works, 1958; later Dr.P.Renault.
534	Tony Shelly/R.A.Gibbons, NZ.	Like many Ds, converted to 3.8-litres early '60s.
535	J.Palacios/Rodolfo Bay, Spain	Now in Le Mans circuit museum.
536	Loyal Katskee, USA.	*Major rebuild, Ireland.*
537	Mauricio Miranda, S.Salvador.	Burnt out in '57 fire, during servicing; replaced by 549.
538	Jack Ensley, USA.	Still USA?
539	XKSS722, Ronald Hoare, UK.	Converted back to D-type; later to N.Moores coll.
540	John Coombs, Philip Scragg, UK.	Converted to XKSS at works, '58/'59.
541	Roberts Harrison, USA.	Still USA.
542	XKSS754 to USA.	*Spares, USA.*
543	Structure ruined, works fire.	Engine rebuilt & supplied to Tojeiro, '57.
544	Dealer Show car, then spares.	*Reconstruction from glassfibre ''special''.*
545	To USA.	Later Peter Ashworth, UK.
546	To USA.	*Major servicing and spares.*
547	XKSS728 to USA.	Earlier a Dealer Show car.
548	Dealer Show car.	Dismantled by works.
549	Dealer Show car.	Dismantled, then used to replace XKD537.
550	XKSS769 to USA.	Formerly Dealer Show car.
551	G.Sportoletti Baduel, UK.	*Spares and Servicing, UK.*
552	John Manussis, E.Africa.	Later Trinidad and Canada.
553	Jack Ensley, USA.	*Purchased in UK by Lynx, resold to Germany.*
554	To Mexico, then USA.	*Spares and repairs, UK.*
555	XKSS701, USA 'demo' car.	*Major rebuild, Japan.* First XKSS, built experimental dept.
556	Destroyed in fire, '57.	Probably prior to, or during, conv. to XKSS.
557	XKSS760 to Canada	Converted back to sort-of-D-type immediately.
558	To Canada	*Reconstructed from remains, France.*
559	XKSS757 to Hong Kong.	Collection of late Nigel Moores.
560	To USA.	*Reconstruction from remains, UK.*
561	Ecurie Ecosse, Feb '56.	*Minor spares supply, UK.*
562	XKSS725 to USA.	Converted after February '57 fire.
563	XKSS704 to USA.	Converted after February '57 fire.
564	XKSS707 to USA.	*Major rebuild work, UK.* Scotland.
565	Destroyed in fire, '57.	Probably prior to, or during, conv. to XKSS.
566	XKSS763 to USA.	*Spares, USA.*

567	XKSS766 to USA.	Converted after '57 fire.
568	XKSS710 to USA.	*Spares, USA.*
569	XKSS713 to USA.	Harrah collection, Nevada.
570	Dismantled at works.	Never painted.
571	Destroyed in fire, '57.	Probably prior to, or during, conversion to XKSS.
572	XKSS719 to USA.	Later back to UK.
573	Belgian team car '56/'57.	Later on long-term loan for Jaguar works display.
574	Destroyed in fire, '57.	During conversion to XKSS.
575	XKSS716 to Canada.	*Major work, UK.* Raced '82 as "D" by John Harper.
601*	1956 works team car.	Later D.Hamilton, see XKD505 and footnote.
602*	1956 works team car.	Injection car, crashed Le Mans '56; see XKD603.
603*	1956 works team car.	Rebuilt with parts from 602 after accident to both.
604*	1956 works team car.	De Dion suspension fitted; crashed & dismantled.
605*	1956 works team car.	Loaned first to Cunningham team, later Turin museum.
606*	1956 works team car.	*Major rebuild work, France.* 1957 Le Mans winner.

Footnote on D-types and XKSSs

The extent of Lynx Engineering's commitment to D-type work is seen clearly from the foregoing. Involvement to a lesser or greater degree with 35 of the 87 numbered cars gives Lynx unrivalled recent experience. When the last two Lynx copy-cars are completed, 22 of them will have been made.

Information in the right-hand column consists of Guy Black's and the author's notes, and does *not* take into account all aspects of identity as specified in the left-hand column.

An asterisk(*) indicates "long-nose" bodywork when new. At the time of writing there is some confusion in the author's mind about the connection between three of these cars – XKD504, XKD505, and XKD601. This confusion goes right back to Jaguar many years ago, when damaged cars had to be cannibalised. In 1958, Duncan Hamilton crashed his ex-works car XKD601 badly at Le Mans; the car was returned to the works experimental department for rebuilding. (It was now virtually two years since Jaguar had stopped racing as a works team, but the factory did still possess XKD505, the 1955 Le Mans winner). Although the degree of cannibalisation is not certain (so far), it seems likely that parts of XKD505 went into the rebuild including (perhaps?) the monocoque centre section. Since 1958, the car's identity has remained strange; whether it is XKD505 or 601 – the car is in the Midland Motor Museum – it is a genuine works car, put together by the works. (Well, *I* think it is). A little later, in the 1960s, XKD504 (then owned by Peter Sutcliffe) appeared below my office window at Browns Lane, badly biffed...a sorry sight. If I had followed its rebuild properly then, I'd know the answer to this question: Was the subframe of 505 still lingering in the experimental department? It seems it was, because, during a rebuild of 504 recently, Guy Black found the number "505" stamped on the subframe! 504 now has a new frame, and "505" (the subframe only) was being built into a "new" long-nose D-type when this book went to press. Was Henry Ford right about history? They say he was misquoted ....

It should be added that there seem to be two "1957 Le Mans winners" now, if not more. (That car *was* XKD606, by the way).

Up to July 1983, I shall be pleased to correspond with anyone who has new or constructive information for the D-type appendix of the major history to be published early in 1984.

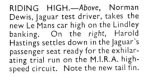

ROAD TESTS

The Motor

656

June 2, 1954

Foretaste of Le Mans

High-speed Impressions of the New Jaguar

By Harold Hastings
Midland Editor

RIDING HIGH.—*Above*, Norman Dewis, Jaguar test driver, takes the new Le Mans car high on the Lindley banking. On the *right*, Harold Hastings settles down in the Jaguar's passenger seat ready for the exhilarating trial run on the M.I.R.A. high-speed circuit. Note the new tail fin.

THE wind is still singing in my ears as I write this and I have only to close my eyes to see a narrow strip of steep banking curving towards me with the slightly unreal speed of a film taken from a low-flying aircraft.

If it were not for the physical sensations of weighing several stone more than the slot machines tell me I really weigh and of the ever-increasing pressure of the wind as the engine speed went up by nearly a thousand revs. on the short straights, the analogy would be almost exact because I have never had a smoother high-speed ride or a steadier one.

These characteristics are the outstanding impressions of some fast laps of the new M.I.R.A. high-speed circuit with Norman Dewis, head tester of Jaguar in one of the new cars which will run at Le Mans next week.

I had already examined the car in detail at the Jaguar works some weeks before when preparing a description of it (*The Motor*, May 12), and that had given me a shrewd idea of its potential. I accordingly jumped at the sudden chance of a ride at M.I.R.A. on the recent opening day.

In the Wind

I was not dressed for this sort of thing and the Jaguar has no screen on the passenger's side, the seat, in fact, normally being completely faired in with a quickly detachable cover secured by Dzus fasteners. "I can lend you a crash hat and visor if you like," offered Dewis, "but if you're not careful, you'll find the wind gets underneath it and pushes your head back." Climbing in through the hatchway and sliding down until my knees were well hunched up, I found that only my eyes and the top of my head were above the 32-in.-high top of the scuttle. I declined the visor but accepted a beret kindly offered by a bystander.

Glasses are a nuisance on these occasions, but by grasping the side pieces
B28

and the edges of the beret, I reckoned I should get by. I did, but my fingers still ache from the effort. At over 150 m.p.h. the wind becomes a positive thing that tugs and whistles at anything so unstreamlined as ears and knuckles.

With an O.K. from a track official we were away up the half mile of straight remaining before the east turn. Busy settling in, I did not notice (shameful as it is for a journalist to have to admit it) what revs. Dewis reached in the gears, but I was most emphatically conscious of the tremendous acceleration which the 250-odd b.h.p. of the latest engine imparts to this lower, lighter and shorter version of the Jaguar. Clutch and gearchange, too, must be above reproach because the overall impression was one of a smooth, continuous surge forward.

Round the banking, the rev. counter was showing 4,300 r.p.m. which, with the axle ratio used on that occasion, represents some 126 m.p.h. Travelling high, but still comfortably below the safety fence, the car was rock steady and, what was even more impressive to one with memories of watching racing cars snaking towards him from the Byfleet Bridge over the old Brooklands track, absolutely stable directionally. Only being pressed downwards and sideways on the seat as lateral "G" came into play gave a true sensa-

tion of the real speed. Perhaps it was this quite remarkable absence of any trace of sway which made the M.I.R.A. banking seem less narrow than I expected in comparison with both Brooklands and Montlhèry.

On the straights, the revs. leapt up in what seemed no time at all to 5,300, which is the equivalent to 156 m.p.h. Here, the tremendous wind pressure on my unscreened head was the only indication of a rise of some 30 m.p.h. The Jaguar remained rock steady and, sighting a distant point along the smooth bonnet, Euclid's definition of a straight line floated oddly through my mind. There was no suggestion of effort on the part of the engine, which remained almost uncannily smooth.

No timing was done, but I suppose our lap speed must have been a little short of 140 m.p.h. When one remembers that Norman Dewis has lapped this same 2.8-mile circuit at nearly 10 m.p.h. faster than that (involving a speed of approximately 170 m.p.h. on the straights) one appreciates something of the true potentialities of this latest Jaguar.

One further impression remains—as we pulled into the tuning bay just after the south turn. The new Le Mans Jaguar stops as rapidly, as smoothly and as positively as it seems to do everything else.

AUTOSPORT, FEBRUARY 11, 1955

JOHN BOLSTER TRIES OUT
The D-Type
JAGUAR

Most statements are open to argument, but this one is not: The D-Type Jaguar is Britain's fastest car, period. For proof, take Le Mans, 1954, and the race-long struggle between the Rolt/Hamilton Jaguar and the Gonzalez/Trintignant 4.9-litre Ferrari. If there is another car in this tight little island that can average 105 m.p.h. for 24 hours on that streaming wet course, I'll eat my deerstalker.

It was thus with a metaphorical grin from ear to ear that I set off for Byfleet to interview this famous machine. There she stood, in a rather exclusive showroom, cheek by jowl with Rolls-Royces, Bentleys and the odd Daimler or so. Her new owner, Duncan Hamilton, was busy selling cars through two telephones at once to the nobility and gentry. "Take her away and enjoy yourself, boy," said he, " but don't drive at much over 165 m.p.h. because she's got the low cog in at the moment." So saying, he pressed the button, and the dead cold engine sprang to life and ticked over evenly and quietly.

The seat fitted Bolster like a glove. At first, the pedals seemed small and close together, an impression that vanished almost at once. The steering wheel was also small, in fact the whole car seemed incredibly low and tiny for a 3½-litre. One sits right down inside the aerodynamic body, and the wrap-around windscreen affords such protection that I did not wear an overcoat on that January morning.

Like all Jaguars, the D-Type has a wonderfully smooth engine. It has, in fact, perfect traffic manners, and can be used for shopping without any thought of its potential performance. There is a passenger's seat, but this is normally covered in the interest of streamlining. The steering is light and responsive, the ultra-close-ratio gearbox could not be easier to handle, and the 7 ft. 6 in. wheelbase and 4 ft. 2 in. track add up

IN BATTLE: Duncan Hamilton in the Jaguar at Le Mans, 1954, where, co-driving with Tony Rolt, he finished second in the G.P. d'Endurance to Gonzalez's 4.9-litre Ferrari.

OKV1, J.D.H. AND J.V.B.: The D-type, its owner and Bolster, sandwiched between two Daimlers at the Byfleet showrooms of Duncan Hamilton.

to a small, nippy vehicle for England's crowded roads.

Did I say nippy? Let's open the six throttles in the Weber carburetters and feel 250 b.h.p. at work! The rear-end skittishness of the C-Type has been eliminated, and once one is out of bottom gear, wheelspin is no longer a problem. The acceleration is deceptive, because it is just one smooth rush. The exhaust note is by no means obtrusive, and the once-magic century has come and gone before one engages top gear with the gentle pressure of a thumb and finger. Then, road conditions alone determine the speed, and mere words cannot describe the sheer ease of the whole performance.

As 120 m.p.h. is there for the asking on any short straight, there is work for the brakes to do. The famous disc brakes are immensely powerful, and, of course, they are more than adequate for the hardest driving. What is more important, though, is the fact that they are entirely progressive, and one feels at home with them immediately. In spite of their power, there is no danger of misjudging their potency. Below 10 m.p.h. they emit a slightly metallic sound, but in normal use they are completely silent.

The steering of the D-Type is light and accurate, nor is one kept so busy at the wheel as in the case of the C-. It feels a much smaller and lighter car than its predecessor, as indeed it is; and its shape gives the driver something to aim. At low speeds, the suspension is fairly firm, but the ride smooths out completely as the Jaguar gets into its stride.

Unfortunately, the shortness of my

250 B.H.P.: The six-cylinder, twin o.h.c. engine, with its three Weber carburetters, adequately fills the bonnet of the D-type. The oil tank feeds direct to the dry sump engine.

trial precluded the taking of performance figures, but one hopes that this model may be submitted for a full road test later on. In the meantime, the lap speed at Le Mans gives an indication of the sort of urge that it possesses. What no figures show, however, is the indefinable feeling of *quality* that this machine imparts. I am in the lucky position to sample many successful competition cars. Although such vehicles always show high performance, it is frequently accompanied by roughness and intractability, plus some odd rattles and the drumming of body panels. The Jaguar, on the other hand, gives that same air of breeding which the XK coupé possesses. It is, indeed, a new conception in sports-racing cars.

I do not approve of the possession of very fast cars by inexperienced drivers, but I feel that this is one of the easiest of the real flyers to handle. Unlike some of the latest speed models, it does allow some margin for error, and there is nothing tricky about it. Obviously, its full potentialities on a road circuit can only be extracted by the higher echelon of racing drivers, but one's nearest and dearest could drive it through the West End without demur.

There remains the usual Jaguar miracle, which is the price. How they turn the thing out for a basic £1,895 I am frankly unable to imagine. I can only say that one can pay very much more for a great deal less—and leave it at that!

Handling Impressions and Performance— 0–100 m.p.h. in 14 sec.

Jaguar XK SS

A large curved screen, fixed side shields and hood together give good protection against wind and rain. The whole bonnet, strap retained, hinges forward

JUST over two years ago, colleague Michael Clayton had the opportunity to drive a C-type Jaguar, later to describe his experiences in print. His patient passenger that day, I eventually persuaded him to let me take over at the wheel, but by then it was almost dark, and raining hard. Memories of that night came back again recently when one evening I found myself in temporary possession of a later and even more potent product of the same factory, a Jaguar XK SS.

Whatever the cars one has been fortunate enough to drive, anything of the nature of the XK SS never fails to produce a thrill. Delightful as the eager small cars can be, a big, powerful engine has the advantage every time when one wants to taste the delights of real high-speed motoring. In this particular case, too, there was the added appeal that the car is, for the time being, unique, and to drive it is something of a privilege.

Getting into the driving seat presents no particular problems. The diminutive door allows one to step over the sill; even if there were any difficulty in getting down behind this particular steering wheel, it is unlikely that any right-thinking person would complain. The deeply padded driving seat has a sharply curved backrest to hold the driver without producing any feeling of restriction. The seat cushion gives comfortable support beneath the thighs, and the door and side screen do not curtail arm movement. No seat adjustment is provided—such a car is better "made to measure."

I have noticed before that with bodywork of this kind, where the seat and steering column are not adjustable for length, drivers of differing heights can still be comfortable. There are, of course, limits as far as the distance between the pedals and seat is concerned. The XK SS driving position, to my knowledge, seemed to suit three men of very different stature and the car was also driven by a woman who, however, preferred to have a cushion behind her.

The well-curved screen is high enough to give ample protection, goggles being unnecessary. Instruments are kept to essentials—they consist of large diameter rev. counter and speedometer on the left side of the column, with oil pressure gauge and coolant temperature gauge to the right. The direction indicator switch is also on the right, with a green warning light, and the horn button is by the door pillar where it can be conveniently pressed by one's knee. A small cubby hole with sufficient room for iron rations on a long drive (the tank holds 37 Imp. gallons) faces the passenger.

Anybody fortunate enough to occupy the passenger seat must have short legs to be comfortable. The seat itself matches its opposite number for support, but legroom is severely restricted. It is surprising how small an enthusiast can make himself when offered a ride in a car like this Jaguar!

There is nothing tricky about starting up. A normal ignition switch with a key is fitted above the large diameter starter button. One push on the button and the car comes to life—alive with the throbbing of the exhaust from the twin pipes just in front of the left rear wheel; alive with the slight vibration—no more than a tickle—felt through the floor and seat. There is a brief, harsh, mechanical signal and whine from under the bonnet, which smoothes out as soon as the r.p.m. increase. The needle of the chronometric rev counter stabs up towards the red caution line at 5,800 r.p.m., when the engine is blipped to check for hesitation.

Clutch pedal movement is fairly short, and against more than average pressure, but the clutch had no vices. It is definitely either in or out, but there is no snatch or jerky take-off. On this particular occasion the clutch was not on its best behaviour and there was slight slip. It was not possible to spin the rear wheels on getaway on a dry surface, as could normally be done.

In spite of this, it was possible to record a few highly impressive acceleration figures against the stop watch. The average time for the standing quarter mile was 14.3 sec, the speed reached being almost 100 m.p.h. From rest to 70, 100 and 120 m.p.h. the times were 7.5, 14.4, and 19.7 sec respectively. In top gear the time from 40 to 60 m.p.h. was 5.5 sec, 60 to 80

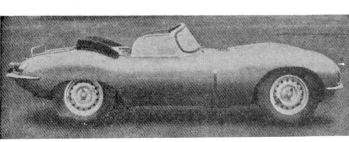

Despite the addition of road equipment, including bumpers and luggage rack, the XK SS appears handsome and well balanced. Length is 14ft and height, at base of screen, 2ft 7½in

m.p.h. 6 sec, and 80 to 100 m.p.h. 5 sec. At about 4,000 r.p.m. the power comes in so hard that a driver or passenger not accustomed to the car feels that he is perhaps in some rocket-propelled sledge.

With the 3.54 to 1 axle fitted to this car, maximum speeds in first, second, third and top gears are estimated by the makers to be 66, 85, 109 and 144 m.p.h. at 6,000 r.p.m. This gives a figure of 24 m.p.h. per 1,000 r.p.m. in top. Four other axle ratios are available: 2.93, 3.31, 3.92 and 4.09.

The car's natural gait for steady driving is 20 to 30 m.p.h. higher than for fast cruising in a less ambitious sports car. On the open road, driving in comfort and without haste, 100 to 120 m.p.h. showed on the speedometer on each clear straight, and yet the braking power was such that the car nosed into successive bends at 60 to 70 m.p.h. without apparent braking effort after the bursts of speed. Just as impressive as the breathtaking acceleration is this smooth power of the brakes.

Fuel consumption depends a great deal on how the car is driven, but the D-types, which are very near relations. managed approximately 12 m.p.g. at Le Mans and the SS, driven normally on the roads, is capable of at least 18 m.p.g.

The steering is very light and high geared, so that the tendency of the inexperienced is to be clumsy with it. At speeds of more than 100 m.p.h. on rough roads or cambered edges a contradictory "grip lightly" technique is required, to give the requisite precise guidance without being heavy handed. Normal cornering as such seems to call for less delicacy of touch than driving straight on not-too-good surfaces. This quality, and the need to "float" the steering, the XK SS shares with Grand Prix cars.

Subdued Noise, Comfort

The wind noise and the general effects of the engine and exhaust are not nearly so fierce as one might imagine or as they are remembered from earlier experience with the C type, which had only a racing screen. When the XK SS gets really wound up, the occupants feel even more a part of the car, for a warm blanket of air wraps the cockpit and the cold slipstream rushes around the shapely contours, avoiding the interior like a static charge.

Like most race-bred cars, the XK SS is superbly controllable and safe. These qualities were demonstrated during the later part of a drive when it started to rain heavily. The wipers were switched on, and, like cut-throat razors, quickly swept the screen clear. The first experience with the car had been in the dark a few days previously; then the screen was covered with flies and the head lamps pointed skywards. This time a few drops of rain were not going to be allowed to interfere with my enjoyment, although caution was the word.

Now, on the wet tarmac, the power readily spun the wheels, and pressing the throttle a little harder at an indicated 100 m.p.h. on the accurate speedometer would cause the back of the car to wag. The wooden-rimmed steering wheel was allowed to float lightly between my hands. and the car assumed an arrow-like course

Out on a damp evening in Warwickshire—the trade plates are a temporary attachment. The car is exceptionally low but has good ground clearance. The exhaust outlet is below the passenger door

without lessening speed. To the chorus of wind and exhaust noise was added the whine of the Dunlop R.1 racing tyres which seemed to seal the car to the road.

With so little weight—under 1 ton—and so much power available, there was no real necessity for constant gear changing. Because of the weather conditions, however, the box was used to slow the car more than might have been done had the roads been dry. The gear change was slightly stiff but the lever movements are precise and short between each ratio. First gear has synchromesh, like the rest.

The speed of the car could almost be controlled by the gear box without resort to the Dunlop disc brakes—the most powerful set I have encountered. Triple pairs of pads on the front and a double pair for the rear brakes produced tremendous fade-free stopping power. When applied at slow speeds with discs cold, there was a fair amount of squeal but this disappeared when they were applied hard. The pedal pressure is very light even for maximum effect, and the brakes could be

applied firmly on wet surfaces with confidence.

It is difficult not to run out of superlatives when describing such a car. The steering, light and extremely accurate as already mentioned, has understeer built into the design; slight kick-back can be felt from the road wheels. The suspension is firm without being harsh, and there is no sensation of roll on tight corners.

Outstanding memories of my short experience of the car include the tremendous push in the back when accelerating hard; other traffic appears ahead, is overtaken and fades away in the mirror as if projected in the opposite direction. Also, the steering and roadholding qualities are such that they tend to take care of the shortcomings of a driver new to the car.

The Jaguar XK SS is a true-blue sports car, in so much as it has racing characteristics with touring equipment. As such, it naturally has much more performance, safety and appeal than the run of sports cars—and in America it costs only $5,600.

H. C. F. H.

Left: Black leather trim and upholstery add finish and comfort, but the cockpit remains functionally simple. Small, hinge-down doors help in getting in or out. Right: Note the petrol filler (37 gallons), the footrest on the clutch side

THE XK-SS SOLVES THE TRAFFIC PROBLEM

Speedier cars may be the answer to Britain's overcrowded highways. The faster the car, the sooner it vacates road space for others. With this in mind, Russell Brockbank and J. B. Boothroyd recently took out a Jaguar XK-SS and a flattering amount of short term life insurance

"I see the leaves are on the turn."

RESIDENTS on the test route will not need telling that we followed the line Guildford-Winchester-Salisbury. They will remember us.

There is only one of these motor cars in England, the rest having run off the edge, got stuck under milk tankers, or gone to America, where longer, wider and straighter roads, with fewer tractors towing hay wagons in the middle of them, enable short bursts or maximum speed to be achieved until such time as the police can organize road blocks ahead by short wave. As no more are to be made we had the additional satisfaction of knowing that we were testing the fastest museum piece in existence. The passenger, in particular, found such additional satisfaction welcome. He could do with some. His accommodation was grudging and limited, gouged out of the surrounding mass like a small hole in stiff, hot porridge (the exhaust system travels up his left leg before clotting on the car's left side exterior). His share of the dash cuts him sharply below the kneecaps, or, later, when cringing sets in with the legs well drawn up, across the shinbone. The hand brake will be found to fit conveniently up his right sleeve. The driver, if his shoes aren't too wide, finds no difficulty in depressing the control pedals independently of each other, and can comfortably extend his legs to a squatting position. Over 100 miles per hour he feels the cold, and wonders if there is any quick way of transferring half a dozen hot pipes to his side of the car.

There are four hooter buttons, two of which are sited near the gearshift and tend to be sounded simultaneously with the change—just when, in fact, warning of approach is not needed. It was found wise in our case, when the passenger often wanted to hoot as well, to come to an agreement on whose fingers should fly to which button. This worked well, particularly as the driver tended to use the one in the center of the wheel, which, as it happened, wasn't one.

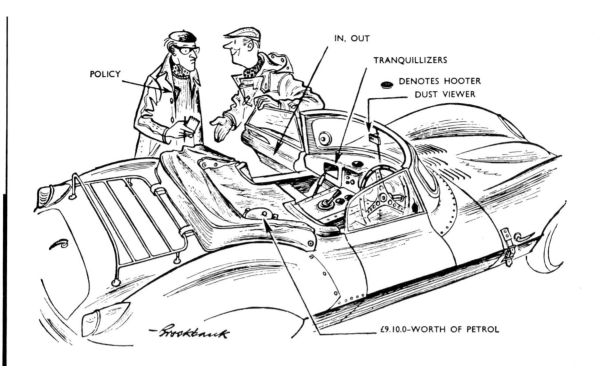

POLICY

IN, OUT

TRANQUILLIZERS

● DENOTES HOOTER
DUST VIEWER

—Brockbank

£9.10.0—WORTH OF PETROL

There is no luggage accommodation. Space which might otherwise be handy for trunks, folding perambulators, playpens, sacks of lawn sand and the like is given over to 38 gallons of fuel. The model tested was in British Post Office red, with damp hand prints on the passenger's door.

It was a fine autumn morning with a crispness in the air when, with dry roads and lips, we took off in a south-westerly direction. We at once entered Hampshire, 12 miles distant, at 96 mph, and changed into top. By this time the portion of the passenger projecting above the windshield had the sensation of being embedded in an ice block, though his socks, by way of compensation, were already hot to the touch.

The car was not offensively noisy, so far as it was possible to judge. That is, no adverse criticism was actually heard from scattering road gangs, rocking wayside coffee stalls or a middle-aged couple near Liphook whose picnic was blown up a grass bank. The noise is less a car noise than a pleasing *musique concrete* of wounded bison (engine), nose flutes in ecstasy (tires), and pigs at slaughter (disc brakes); in slow running the orchestration is further added to by spittings on giant flat irons to simulate the six dyspeptic carburetors. This last effect, however, came in only after a rigid throttling down to 70-75 mph to conform to the requirements of built-up area restrictions.

A notable aspect of the test was the good behavior of other motorists noticeable throughout. Even drivers clearly unaccustomed to being overtaken put their curbside wheels on the verge and waved us on just after we had gone past.

Lunch was taken in Salisbury, where some delay was experienced while the passenger, now shaped like an old soup tin pressed for remelting, was pried out by the half-dozen heavy, fresh-faced young men in one-piece caps and fur-collared duffle coats who had been drawn from nearby cars and wished to see, stroke, sniff and otherwise investigate the car. One of these insisted on joining us in the dining room of the Cathedral Hotel, but would neither eat anything nor remove his outer clothing in case we drove away suddenly and robbed him of the spectacle. We tried to turn his conversation from single dry plate clutches and

protected air intakes by asking whether our chosen parking site was police proof, but he dismissed this as meaningless delirium and plunged into some exhaust manifolding on a DB-3-S Aston Martin. He later indulged us by saying that Salisbury was a very pro-motoring city, and never prosecuted cars of over 200 bhp.

On re-entering the car and beginning the return journey it was found that the passenger's lunch was folded up under the breastbone, where it promised to be a lasting obstruction. This proved to have been distributed more equably over the digestive system shortly after Alresford, where a smart piece of braking from 120 mph to a near standstill (58 mph), as a tribute to three busses overtaking two more round a bend, arrested an interesting telescopic lens effect and turned the driver's cap through 360°.

To sum up, the SS isn't everyone's car. Everyone couldn't get in it. It eats up an immense amount of road, converting a 10-mile stretch of straight into something the size of a bus ticket—and thus detracting from the finer points of the scenery. But for the man who wants to leave as much road as empty as possible for other people, who likes to overtake a convoy of six sand-and-gravel trucks with trailers in a space which the ordinary motorist would regard as a tight squeeze for overtaking an elderly lady pushing a bicycle, who doesn't mind having his passenger's shoes on fire and a wife who sits by the telephone with palpitations as soon as the sound of his exhaust has died away, it may be said to exhibit certain points of advantage

Reproduced by permission of Punch.

OWNER'S & RESTORER'S VIEW'S

Owner's view

Martin Morris has had more experience of racing his own D-type in modern times than anyone else, and is therefore well qualified to express the active owner's viewpoint.

He is, perhaps, best known for his skilful driving of an ERA single-seater, but he always wanted to race a classic sports car, too. He tried an Aston Martin DB3S before purchasing a C-type Jaguar – a car which he still possesses as well as the D-type.

His D-type, XKD404, was usually registered OKV 3. Formerly a works car, it had given the D-type its first-ever race win driven by the late Ken Wharton and Peter Whitehead in the 1954 Reims 12-hour. It had been sold and spent a period abroad, where its best result was John Love's victory in the 1960 Grand Prix of Angola. In the early 1970s it was back in the UK, purchased by John Melville-Smith and partially restored at the Jaguar works. Morris raced the car while it was owned by Melville-Smith, purchasing it after an unfortunate accident at Snetterton.

Martin Morris takes up the story: "The first time I ever drove the car I thought: Fabulous! – no one can possibily beat me! I was quite wrong, of course, but it does feel fantastic to drive. I'd raced the car for several seasons before the prang. The brakes were always a problem in those days. Sometimes you had total loss of 'pedal' due to pad 'knock-off', and there was too much rear bias. Afterwards I felt no confidence in the braking system and converted it to a modern one with twin master cylinders, adjustable balance bar, small 4-pot calipers and no servo. The diameter of the discs was reduced from $12\frac{3}{4}$ to 12 inches and we put in extra cooling ducts. This has worked well, and given peace of mind, but it is less powerful than the original system; I still have the original components and could convert back."

This is a good point. To race a D-type seriously today *should* mean using modern components such as wheels, brake and tyres, from a safety point of view. Most regulations and attitudes in historic car racing reflect enlightenment. Everyone likes to see historic cars race; no one likes to see them badly damaged – internally or externally. Martin Morris recalls his own accident:

"The car is immensely strong and I was totally protected in the cockpit area. The car rolled after impact and the tailfin/headrest acted as a rollover bar – otherwise I'd not be here to tell you about it! After stripping out to the bare frame and monocoque it all went on a jig, and from the front to the rear of the monocoque, the maximum 'out-of-true' was $\frac{3}{16}$ inch. The difficult parts of the rebuild – re-skinning the nearside of the monocoque, repairing the frame, tail, and bonnet – were done by G.P. Metalcraft. I did the mechanical side, the modifications to the brakes, and some suspension changes to match the handling to my old-fashioned driving."

Martin Morris has driven the D-type in two historic Le Mans races and even at Laguna Seca in California besides regular appearances in Britain, and is a great believer in using it as a road car:

"We never use a trailer because I can't resist driving the car. In California and in France OKV 3 has been used for touring and picnics. There's plenty of luggage space if you take out the spare wheel! I drive with the old-style windscreen, but there's a second screen for my wife, Sue – or me when she's driving. She enjoys the car too. You notice the car's good shape on motorways – abroad, of course – where you can squirt up to 130 odd then coast for miles!"

Martin Morris has a 3.8-litre engine, as well as the 3.4 which is, of course, the correct size for the car. Bryan Wills of Newton Abbot is, he says, "the best engine builder I know", and he also recommends the work of John Pearson and Jim Abbott from personal experience.

From my experience of driving D-types, I share Martin Morris's enthusiasm for them as road cars. On the other hand, the passenger legroom is so limited that it takes a very short person to be comfortable on the nearside – as described so graphically in the *Punch* story reprinted in this book.

Restorer's view

As the man more involved in D-type rebuilds than anyone else, Guy Black, of Lynx Engineering, is known to all owners, and his comments are essential for anyone aspiring to ownership.

Since his first Jaguar rebuild he has been involved with the restoration of fifteen more, *and* made three faithful C-type copies besides.

The last of 22 Lynx cars (D-type appearance, E-type mechanically) were being put into production when this book went to press. Quite apart from these, Guy Black has so far organised the rebuilding, servicing, or supply of spares for 35 D-types (identified by chassis number in this book).

What does Guy Black have to say about the D-type's basic design?

"The whole concept of the 'D' is quite fascinating from an engineering point of view, combining aircraft engineering and design with highly developed production engineering. The result is a very effective, mass-produced racing car which is also immensely strong, simple and without interchangeability problems, making life quite easy if restoring D-types is your living – though some items such as the complicated braking system, the special chassis tubing, multi-plate clutch and the gearbox do provide problems. We found Jaguar Cars Ltd immensely helpful in providing spares (when found and available), drawings, technical and archive information, and general encouragement."

On the subject of rebuild problems, he comments:

"A number of D-types had their engines removed in the States and V8s fitted instead. This conversion usually means the chassis was butchered, sometimes the suspension; and if the 'D' gearbox was still in place it was grossly over-stressed. Gearboxes are particularly difficult to overhaul as there are virtually no items in them common to any other Jaguar gearbox, so with spares now virtually unobtainable we have to make everything. I think there is now no item that we have not made and, in fact, we have even made complete gearboxes. I don't think many people realise just how few items on the D-type are interchangeable with production Jaguar components. Apart from minor items like nuts and bolts, the only major item that is unaltered is the timing cover on the engine; even the cylinder block is different. Lying over at 8°, the engine to gearbox mounting flange is thus assymmetrical. A few of the original suppliers of 'D' components do help us still, though most find it slightly inconvenient supplying small quantities. In most instances we have had to reproduce spares ourselves; when we do this we go to great lengths to ensure they are totally authentic and indistinguishable from the original item."

Finally, on the question of authenticity and identity of a car which possesses two separable chassis components – the front subframe and the monocoque centre section – Guy Black clarifies the situation this way:

"A D-type could be restored from just a handful of tubes (with chassis number!) if required. There is virtually nothing we cannot supply now, though sometimes it is difficult to justify calling a car built thus, original. This is becoming an increasing problem now that these cars have become so valuable. Our own criteria are based on the chassis (or remains) having a continous history from new. It is sometimes rather difficult to decide which car is what, if you are presented with a car's obviously original chassis when you know the car exists already with an original replacement chassis in it! In English Law a car's identity is with the chassis and number, not necessarily on its continuous history. Morally speaking however, the remaining 'mass' of the car may represent the continous history. Quite a problem! If nothing else, one can safely say that there will be no reduction in the number of surviving D-types, and probably the reverse!"

CLUBS, SPECIALISTS & BOOKS

Clubs

The D-type and the XKSS, and even the copies of same, are rare in any company and always the star displays at any club gathering.

Anyone ferreting for a D-type is sure to find that there is an expert on the subject within his or her national historic car club, if not in the nearest Jaguar club. As there are so few owners, information and experience are usually shared as part of the pleasure of ownership – though there are exceptions to every rule, of course.

The most appropriate sections of the Jaguar Drivers Club in the UK would be the XK Register – the D-type was often referred to at the works as the "XK 120D" – and the E-type Register which is more appropriate to Deetype and Lynx owners.

In North America, there is a central organisation of officially recognised Jaguar clubs, and it will supply information on regional activities.

In most countries, the whereabouts or availability of any D-type or derivative does not take long to establish.

Jaguar Drivers Club Ltd.
Rosemary Hinton,
Headquarters Secretary,
Jaguar House;
18 Stuart Street,
Luton,
Bedfordshire,
England

XK Register
Richard Wood,
81 East Avenue,
Talbot Woods,
Bournemouth,
Dorset,
England

E-type Register
George Gibbs,
Burghclere Grange School,
near Newbury,
Berkshire,
England

Jaguar Clubs of North America, Inc.
Michael Cook,
Headquarters Secretary,
600 Willow Tree Road,
Leonia,
New Jersey, 07605,
USA

Classic Jaguar Association
Jack Rabell,
President,
2860 West Victoria Drive,
Alpine,
California, 92001,
USA

Specialists

Wherever there are historic motor cars, some professional specialists have built up a reputation for the (usually high) quality of their work.

Most of the specialists in D-types – real and imitation – are in the UK, where there is a Jaguar Specialists Association.

At the time of writing, this organisation has eighteen members, who got together because of their feeling that the Jaguar marque had attracted more than its fair share of so-called "specialists", with the result that complaints about unsatisfactory work were on the increase. This association of established businesses – several of which are run by former Jaguar employees – is intended to eliminate the customer's problems as far as possible. The Association claims that its aims and objectives are "to maintain a high standard of service, restoration and parts supply, and to protect the interests of Jaguar owners, especially those with obsolete models".

The Jaguar Specialists Association is quite separate from the dealer network of Jaguar Cars Limited, but the company does provide an observer – as does the Jaguar Drivers Club. As suggested in the text, there *are* experts who are *not* members of the JSA. The following are the JSA members likely to be able to help D-type owners on matters of reconstruction and authenticity, and each will probably offer good advice in response to genuine enquiries. The author, who is not a member, will try to do so too, especially on historical matters (letters can be forwarded by the publisher).

Classic Autos
10 High Street,
Kings Langley,
Hertfordshire,
England.
(09277-62994)

Aubrey Finburgh has a wealth of experience in the refabrication of perspex screens, major and minor body panelwork, the rebuilding of instruments, and all types of mechanical work.

Classic Power Units
18 Trevor Close,
Tile Hill,
Coventry,
England.
(0203-461136)

Engine rebuilding and servicing by George Hodge, for many years the competition engine builder in

Jaguar's customer service department.

Deetype Replicas
South Gibcracks Farm,
Bicknacre Road,
East Hanningfield,
Chelmsford,
Essex,
England.
(0245-415380)

Bryan Wingfield wishes he hadn't used the term "Replica" in the name of his company, which makes new cars in the style and spirit of the C-type and D-type.

D.K. Engineering
10-16 Hallowell Road,
Northwood,
Middlesex,
England.
(09274-21399)

David Cottingham and his staff have been renovating and rebuilding exotic or interesting cars for many years, and were responsible for putting two of the later Lynxes together, in association with DCM (former Lynx sales agents).

Forward Engineering
Barston,
near Solihull,
West Midlands,
England.
(06755-2163/2530)

Ron Beaty was a Jaguar apprentice and then an engineer in the factory's experimental department before setting up on his own in the mid 1960s. His competition engines are used in cars and boats – and even for the sport of tractor-pulling.

Alan R. George
11 Small Firms' Compound,
Dodwells Bridge Estate,
Hinckley,
Leicestershire,
England.
(0455-615937)

Another former Jaguar works man, Alan George specialises in gearbox

rebuilds, although of course the D-type is a difficult one for parts.

Lynx Engineering
Castleham Estate,
St. Leonards-on-sea,
East Sussex,
England.
(0424-51277)

Guy Black and Chris Keith-Lucas direct the mechanical and body restoration, and even full reconstructions, of C-type and D-type Jaguars. They also created the E-type-based Lynx car, which looks like a D-type. This model was sold fully built and sometimes in component form.

Phillips Garage
103/7 New Canal Street,
Digbeth,
Birmingham,
England.
(021-6430912)

Harry Phillips is a service, repair, and exchange engine specialist and, probably of more interest to D-type owners, secretary of the Jaguar Specialists Association.

R.S. Panels
Kelsey Close,
Attleborough Fields Estate,
Nuneaton,
England.
(0203-388572/89561)

Bob Smith and his team manufacture panels and complete bodies of all kinds, including those for D-types *and* Lynxes.

Note: Membership of the JSA is not relevant for everyone, and at least two well-known companies mentioned in the text should be mentioned here, too. They are:

Grand Prix Metalcraft
2-3 Thane Works,
Thane Villas,

London N.7
England.
(01-609-0389/0384)

Peter Hingerton runs this company which has rebuilt D-types, and supplied Deetype Replicas with their last ten bodies.

Williams and Pritchard Ltd.
25 First Avenue,
Edmonton,
London N.18,
England.
(01-807-6559)

This was the first company to rebuild D-types in a big way and made the first four bodies for Deetype (including the prototype) – *and* the prototype Lynx body.

Books

This is the first hardback book on the specific subject of the D-type. An owners' instruction manual was published by the factory, but it's not easy to find one now. In any case, more than a quarter of a century on from the car's heyday, the practical advice of specialists and other owners is likely to be of most use to the newcomer.

The model's background is covered by Paul Skilleter's prize-winning **Jaguar Sports Cars** (Haynes/Foulis) and Chris Harvey's well-illustrated **Jaguars in Competition** (Osprey). However, the definitive work on the D-type/XKSS and its successors in motorsport is **Jaguar Sports Racing and Works Competition Cars from 1954** (Haynes/Foulis), which will be published in 1984.

PHOTO GALLERY

1

2

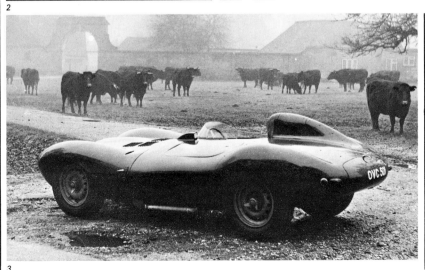

3

1. Windcheater: The unnamed Jaguar prototype photographed beside the Belgian motorway in October 1953, when it touched 180mph driven by Norman Dewis who just managed to peer out from under the cockpit canopy to see the road ahead. The famous fitters are 'Dunlop Mac' (left) and Joe Sutton of Jaguar. Between them is the man responsible for the D-type and E-type shapes, Malcolm Sayer, who called this car the 'XK120C Mk. II' in his reports.

2. The definitive shape. Smoothly-curving, the first D-type structure nears completion with only the projecting bonnet strap and side-exhaust cowl to mar the effect. (Long-nose cars had rear exhaust.)

3. Early morning light emphasises the shape of the prototype, chassis number XKD 401 (or, originally, XKC 401). This short-nose style was followed almost exactly for the production models.

4

5

6

4. Artwork for the D-type catalogue (yes, it was catalogued) again shows the car's uniqueness. The tailfin was available as an 'optional extra', but the built-in auxiliary lamp was a feature of the first works batch of D-types only.

5. The view of 401 as seen by visitors to the National Motor Museum at Beaulieu, Hampshire, England. The 'tapering' effect is not purely perspective; the D-type was slightly narrower at the rear. Bonnet hump is not quite central/symmetrical because engine in D-type is canted over.

6. Contemporary picture of 401 at the Jaguar works; at the wheel is technical director, Bill Heynes, the man responsible for all Jaguar engineering from 1935 to 1969. Note absence of auxiliary lamp.

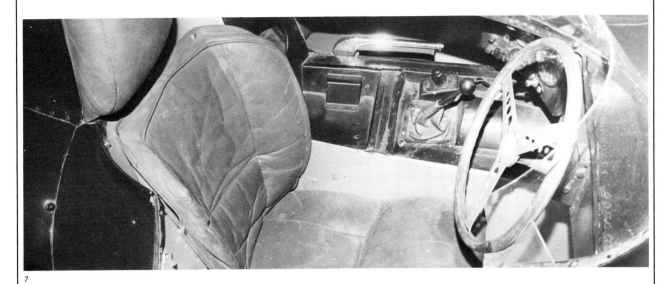

7

7. The next six photographs show detail views of XKD 401, the factory's own prototype, which may be regarded as fairly typical of the first six cars and not dissimilar to the production ones. Comfy cockpit was developed from that of 'bubble' car (see picture 1). To become habitable for 24 hours, it acquired a headrest and fresh air.

8. As Martin Morris has found, with his sister car, removal of spare wheel provides plenty of space for soft luggage! Occasionally, in the early days, boot lids would flop open disconcertingly during racing; standard tweek was to wire the handle to the body.

9. It was always said that the D-type was built around the diminutive Norman Dewis, Jaguar's chief experimental test driver. Bill Heynes isn't exactly tall either; but burlier drivers, notably Mike Hawthorn and Duncan Hamilton, managed. The author takes Size 12s, and has dealt with this pedal box in soft shoes, so it can't be too bad. Note the simple toe and heel rests.

10. Neat and tidy: this shot shows the underbonnet disposition of most components. The original tyres have been replaced with later-type road ones, of course (compare with 6). Chassis number was punched into frame where it formed top shock-absorber mounting, but is only an aid to, not proof of, a typical D-type's identity. In this case, however, it's original!

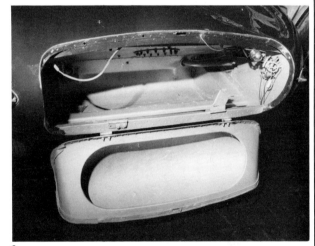

8

9

10

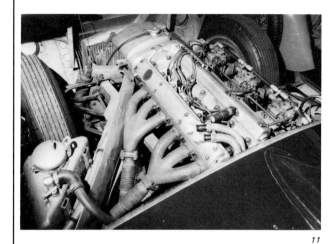

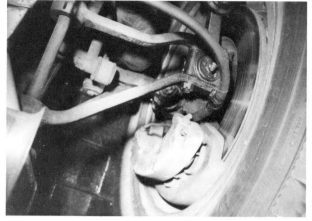

11   12

13

11. Another angle to '401': this shows the dry-sump engine's oil tank in close-up.

12. Triple-pads in front. Some production parts (and many production principles) were used in the D-type ... but genuine replacement parts are hard to come by, nowadays.

13. This is a good example of a production D-type, Chassis No. XKD 573. Originally it had a full-width screen (for Le Mans 1956/7; it came 4th, both times); it started life with the Belgian national team; later it travelled to Japan privately, before being bought by John Coombs, now retired, formerly Jaguar agent and entrant, thanks to whom it is usually on show at the Jaguar works in Coventry. (Car behind is the classic SS Jaguar 100).

14. The following nine photographs illustrate XKD 573. A 'Standard option', the small fin is easily removed, not affecting bootlid.

14

15. Streamlined cowl to mirror.

16. Cockpit shot shows 'production' layout. (Compare with photo 7).

17. Le Mans required the body and wheels to overlap by a certain amount, longitudinally, so these small body extensions were fitted, adjacent to wheelarches, when necessary.

18. Side exhaust tended to spoil clean 'D' lines.

19. Distinctive Dunlop wheel for D-type, later seen on Connaught and others in the Grand Prix field. The works used 16 and sometimes 17 inch road wheels; today's copy-cars use modern tyres; thus they tend to have stronger (alloy/steel) wheels of 15 inches diameter.

15

16

17

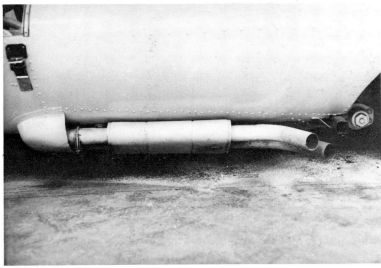

18

19

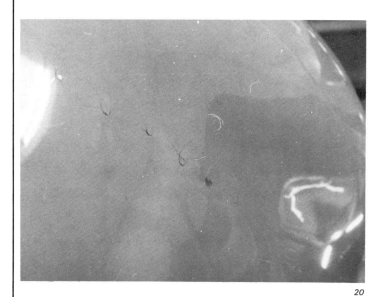

20

20. Alloy bodies move against their rivets; XKD 573 has been tidied-up and repainted several times, but this is the state today (1983) of the area where its flexible fuel tanks are attached.

21. Quick-release fuel tank cap under quick-release fuel tank cap cover in head rest; note how fin blends in.

22. Identification plate of XKD 573 provides clue to original chassis, body, engine, and gearbox combinations. As well as the recommended lubricants, the valve clearances (in inches) are stamped at the bottom: 0.006 inlet (cold) and 0.010 exhaust.

23. Accessibility: with the bonnet hinged forward, everything can be got at handily. The battery is mounted on the offside, outside the main frame member, almost opposite the oil tank.

21

22

23

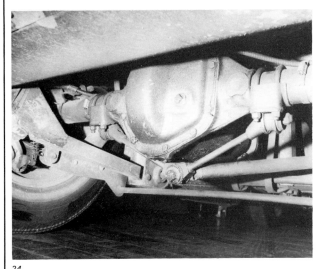

24

25

26

27

24 & 25. Two views of rear end, showing axle location. Note the four trailing arms, and twin-pad brake discs. One picture (25) was taken during the course of assembly and shows two special tools in place.

26. The heart of the matter: Jaguar's XK cylinder head in the rough-cut state, on the Jaguar production line. The hemispherical combustion chamber was a Jaguar characteristic.

27. General view of Jaguar D-type's engine, gearbox, and ancillaries, ready to lift into car.

28. Works 1955 long-nose D-type, photographed when new, on the works sportsfield. The fin extends to the rear of the body, the screen wraps round at a higher level, as 1954 protection had been barely adequate for 24 hours.

28

29

30

29. Another view of a 1955 works car, this time in the colours of the American Jaguar racing team, run by Briggs Cunningham. Note: Le Mans regulation body extensions (to cover tyres) are not yet fitted; also new brake-cooling ducts but no auxiliary light.

30 & 31. Two more recent views of the 1955 Le Mans car. (This is, basically, the 1955 Le Mans winner, XKD 505, though some parts are from XKD 601 which Duncan Hamilton crashed so badly at Le Mans in 1958. This car always creates problems for historians, but it is a very fine example just the same. It lives at the Midland Motor Museum, in the care of Michael Barker; the museum is close to Bridgnorth in Shropshire, England.) The light-coloured intake surround is as per identification of the Mike Hawthorn/Ivor Bueb machine. '2 CPG' was Duncan Hamilton's registration number for XKD 601, and was still used after the 1958's 'reconstruction' – see text. Early in 1983 it was learned that Duncan Hamilton and his son, Adrian, has re-acquired '2 CPG' for posterity.

31

32

33

32. '2 CPG' in close-up. Compare the 'production' dashboard with photo 7 ...

33 ... the passenger seat: as cramped as ever, but that's what the regulations clearly allowed.

34. Distinctly D-type. The water pump's threaded housing which can be screwed down, to correct clearance ...

35. ... and the transmission-driven pump assembly by Plessey.

34

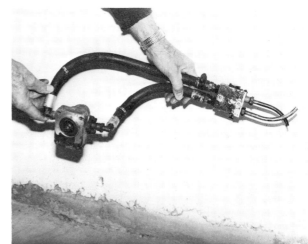

35

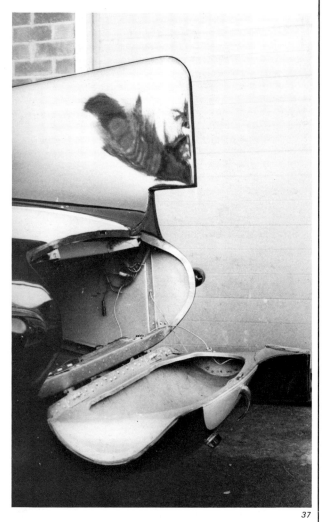

36

37

36 & 37. Two views of 1955 tail, with bigger tailfin, merging more smoothly into the tail of the car, and extended so far back that it had to be incorporated into the bootlid. Note rear tailpipes.

38. Note new oil tank under the bonnet for 1955 works cars.

39. Two and three pad calipers of the regular D-type, with (front, right) a much later type, more likely to be fitted on competitive models in historic racing today.

38

39

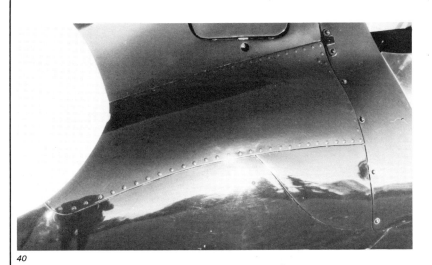

40. Close-up of '2CPG' again, showing the riveted seamline of the long, high tailfin along the rear deck. Here an experimental brake-cooling duct may have been covered, too.

41. A 1956 Le Mans requirement was a full-width screen, so Jaguar reluctantly added to the frontal area of the long-nose D-type like this. Note nearside door.

42. Another close-up from the same occasion (a test session at the Motor Industry Research Association's test track near Nuneaton), showing how Jaguar made the best of a bad job. The regs. had said that the passenger compartment must have a screen too, but not that there had to be a passenger! Note countersunk bonnet strap.

40

41

42

43

44

45

46

43. 1956 car in paddock at Le Mans, mechanic Frank Rainbow at the wheel. This is the car which Jack Fairman crashed early in the race. The little stick-on badge with the word 'Jaguar' (usually on nose and tail of 'D') was red on white. Even a badge protruding from the body would have spoiled the smooth shape.

44. Privateers converted their production D-types to full-width screen, when necessary. This is the Ecurie Ecosse 1956 Le Mans winner, XKD 501, pictured at a commemorative event at Oulton Park a decade later with Graham Birrell at the wheel.

45 & 46. Two close-ups of production D-type XKD 561, as raced by Ecurie Ecosse in 1956, and sold to Maxwell Trimble for 1957. Note position of instrumentation, and higher mirror on windscreen buttress. (These pictures kindly loaned by Max Trimble, seen at the wheel.)

47. Authentic underside. Racing mechanic, Bob Penney, with a works car, giving good view of well-studded sump and lower chassis members.

48. Contemporary production line, alongside Mark Seven saloons at Browns Lane, Coventry. The nature of the structure is very clear here — centre section and (engineless) front subframe form the heart; bonnet and tail sections have no integral role.

47

48

49. The centre section was important to the structure; nevertheless, it was opened out! This is what XKD 402 looked like when on a visit to the works in 1956 while being converted privately into a road car for John ('Jumbo') Goddard who still owns it.

50,51 & 52. Three views of the prototype Jaguar XKSS, built in the winter of 1956/7 from an existing D-type. Fifteen more were made from unsold (and sometimes incomplete) D-types, and a further two converted at the works for existing D-type owners, thus establishing a grand total of eighteen 'official' XKSSs. The 'XKSS' badges for the bonnets were handmade by apprentices as a training exercise. The first time one of these was raced with the hood up, the driver soon came into the pits — nearly asphyxiated. No equivalent road reports were filed, apparently. The fact is, these were dolled-up Ds.

49

50

51

52

53

53. Quick reference. Three short-nose, finless Ds from
the collection of the late Nigel Moores — left to right,
standard production, XKSS (less luggage rack here), and
with wide screen.

54. When is a D not a D? Deetype Replicas Ltd and
Lynx Engineering have done some very good copies —
over 35 in all — in the last decade (to 1983) and, in a
sense, there couldn't be a better tribute to these great
Jaguars. This long-nose Lynx is owned by Bob Smith of
RS Panels, a Nuneaton specialist firm expert in the art of
bodywork construction, from racing cars to hearses! The
'modern' number plate is the most obvious giveaway,
and indicates the age of the E-type which provided the
mechanical basis for the car.

54

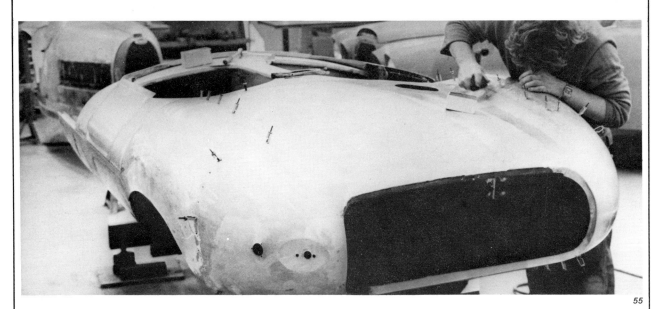

55

56

55. Extensive use of Avdel clips through the rivet holes during the build-up of a tail section at RS Panels.

56. Lynx structure, showing E-type front subframe bolted on to bulkhead. The Deetype is similar, but has a frame extension ('D' style) extending to the back of the cockpit.

57. A virtually new car is built around a D-type subframe bearing the number 'XKD 505' for a Lynx customer; the car which last wore this frame now has a new one. Note the ease with which the works-style tailfin and headrest slips on. Most 'copy' bodies seem to be the long-nose type, but the occasional 'production' and 'XKSS' copies have been made, too.

57

58. One of the most successful participants in the business of historic racing is John Harper who bought this complete reproduction body and frame (which had been to the 1982 Motor Show) from RS Panels, with a view to 're-creating' a particular works car which had independent rear suspension but crashed and was written-off in 1956. A fascinating project, but unfinished at the time of going to press.

58

59

59. Debut for the D-type. 'OKV 1' (XKD 402) shows the scars of an encounter with a slower car which moved across its path. Here it lines up to pass its predecessor (the C-type) which won at Le Mans in 1951 and 1953, and came 4th this time (1954).

60. Same car, same race – the D-type in its first event, Le Mans 1954. After losing much valuable time in the pits, due largely to a clogged fuel filter, Duncan Hamilton and Tony Rolt still took 2nd place, less than two minutes behind the winning Ferrari, after 24 hours of racing.

60

61. First victory. Reims 12-hour race 1954, in which 'OKV 3' (XKD 404) was driven by Ken Wharton (seen here) and Peter Whitehead.

62. Nearly thirty years on, the same car (updated mainly in the braking department) is still a great performer in the hands of Martin Morris, who enjoys it as a road car, too.

61

62

63. Mike Hawthorn leads Juan Manuel Fangio into Tertre Rouge, Le Mans 1955. This epic Jaguar v. Mercedes duel ended when the German team withdrew from the race soon after halftime. (Earlier, a Mercedes had crashed, with many lives lost).

64. Jaguar scored a works 1-2-3 victory in the 1956 Reims 12-hour race, in which the 1955-type windscreens were permitted. This car, shared by Mike Hawthorn and Paul Frere (seen here), led for much of the race; it came second, after team-mate Duncan Hamilton moved ahead and broke the lap record – an act which led to his being sacked from the Jaguar team!

63

64

65. From 1955, Briggs Cunningham entered many races on Jaguar's behalf, though his team was essentially his 'show', run on his money to a great extent. His best driver was undoubtedly Walter Hansgen, seen here winning at Montgomery in 1957. The Cunningham team cars were prepared by Alfred Momo: note the distinctive fin shape he evolved.

65

66

66. David Murray's Ecurie Ecosse team saved the day for Jaguar at Le Mans in 1956, and then came first and second the next year. The 1957 winners were Ron Flockhart and Ivor Bueb (seen here) in this ex-works car prepared by 'Wilkie' Wilkinson. The factory supplied the car's 3.8-litre fuel-injection engine. At least three representations of this car (XKD 606) exist today.

C1

C2

C3

C1. The first D-type, XKD401 (stamped "XKC401" before the car got its type name), at its regular showplace – the National Motor Museum, Beaulieu. It did many test miles but was never actually raced. (Charles Pocklington)

C2. Seen from the nearside, XKD401 shows the auxiliary lamp and side exhaust positions of the first six (1954) D-types. (Charles Pocklington)

C3. 401's well-worn cockpit shows offset instruments of 1954 D-types.

C4

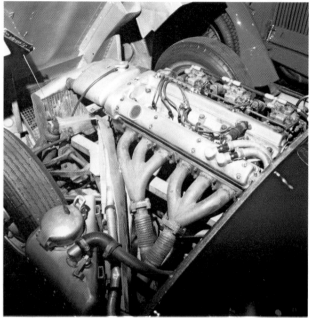

C5

C4, C5 & C6. Three views of 401, showing authentic 1954 underbonnet features, notably the non-detachable front subframe. This unrestored car, still owned by Jaguar, is fitted with road tyres for occasional runs to Coventry, or in the grounds of Beaulieu.

C6

C7

C7. 1955 works 'long-nose' D-type at the Midland
Motor Museum, Bridgnorth. Although a combination of,
probably, two cars (XKD505 and 601) it is nevertheless
a thoroughly authentic machine, little changed since
leaving the works in 1958.

C8. Longer, higher tailfin is exaggerated in this view of
the ex-works, ex-Hamilton car. The aerodynamic
theories of the day ensured plenty of air passed under
the car as well as over it. Stability was such that the D-
type was considered fairly relaxing to drive on the fast
straight at Le Mans.

C8

C9. 2CPG's cockpit with wrap-around screen to give the driver more protection from buffeting in long races. Instruments for 1955 were re-arranged to be read more easily.

C10. The basic design of the D-type never altered, but there were several detail changes, notably (though it can't be shown easily in photographs) the bolting-together of the front subframe and the central monocoque from 1955 on. This shot of 2CPG also shows the squared-off oil-tank top of some works cars, the idea being to get maximum de-aeration of the oil passing through internal baffles. Most cars had the tank which was triangular in plan view; it seemed to work just as well and was not nearly as complicated to make.

C9

C10

C11

C12

C13

C11. At the Jaguar works (on loan from John Coombs) a production D-type, XKD573, is seen with a "Deetype" copy-car. The essentially differing proportions of the standard shape and the 'long-nose' cars can be observed to some extent. The badge on the nose is incorrect.

C12. Despite being rebuilt with 1955-type screen configuration, XKD573 was in fact raced by the Belgian team at Le Mans in 1956 and 1957, coming 4th both times. It was works-prepared: hence (for example) the oil-tank overlapping subframe.

C13. Close-up of nearside front corner of XKD573, showing suspension and brake detail.

C14

C14. The cockpit of XKD573 provides a considerable contrast with that of unrestored XKD401 – and shows many detail differences.

C15. Production car: D-types began to reappear on the circuits in the early 1970s, as historic car racing got under way. As the racing began to get rather serious, so their appearances lessened. It is still possible to see D-types in action though, particularly at the Jaguar Drivers' Club's spring meeting at Silverstone.

C15

C16

C16. Martin Morris with the rebuilt works car, XKD404, at Le Mans for the 1973 historic race in which he came 3rd. (See also cover picture caption).

C17. This D-type was driven to Le Mans in 1973, where it won the historic race, driven by Willie Green. Note full-width Le Mans 56/57 screen; this car, XKD504 did in fact come 2nd at Le Mans in 1957. Ecurie Ecosse cars were first and second that year. The white stripe was the Scottish team's standard identification; other cars had two or three stripes.

C17

C18

C19

C21

C20

C18, C19 & C20. The XKSS, seen head-on, in profile (with a Lister-Jaguar and a D-type bearing a spurious windscreen), and in action on a circuit demonstration in the early '70s by its then owner, Robert Danny.

C21. A "Deetype" visits Jaguar and impresses former works team men Phil Weaver and Frank Rainbow. Phil Weaver (left) took the idea from Bristol aircraft when he produced the oil tank for Jaguar. On the "Deetype" it is just an empty box!